Workbook

THE SANDWICH GENERATION
SURVIVAL GUIDE

Balancing family, finances, and your future

WRITTEN BY *Emily Hutchinson*

A PRACTICAL GUIDE TO SUPPORTING YOUR LOVED ONES WITHOUT SACRIFICING YOUR DREAMS.

Copyright

Emily Hutchinson

About ME

Hi, I'm Emily Hutchinson — a wife, mom of two, and a proud African American woman navigating life in the Sandwich Generation. By day, I serve as a federal employee, and by night, I'm balancing the needs of my family, my marriage, and my own dreams.

I'm the second of five children, which means I learned early what it means to share, to support, and to step up when family needs you. Those lessons have shaped how I care for my loved ones today.

When I'm not working or writing, you'll probably find me crafting — it's my creative outlet and my way of finding peace in the middle of life's chaos.

This book grew out of my real experiences. Like so many in our community, I know what it feels like to stretch yourself between generations — raising kids, supporting parents, and still trying to plan for your own future. My hope is that by sharing what I've learned, I can help others feel less alone and more empowered on this journey.

Content

INTRODUCTION

You are Not Alone

If you've picked up this book, chances are you're tired. Tired of holding everything together — the bills, the kids, the parents, the appointments, the late-night worries. Tired of feeling like you have to be strong for everyone else while wondering who will be strong for you.

This book begins with one truth: you are not alone!

The Silent Struggle

Millions of adults across the country are living exactly what you're living — raising children or supporting adult kids, while at the same time caring for aging parents. This is the invisible load of the **Sandwich Generation.**

But because so much of this work happens quietly — in homes, in hospital rooms, in family group chats — it can feel like nobody else understands. You may think you're failing, when in reality, you're simply carrying more than most people ever see.

Naming the Pressure

In communities of color especially, this pressure comes with **cultural expectations and family duty**. You're expected to be the helper, the provider, the fixer, the one who doesn't say "no." It's a role you may step into out of love, but it can quickly become overwhelming.

The truth is: there is no shame in feeling exhausted. There is no weakness in admitting it's hard. The weight you carry is real, and it deserves to be acknowledged.

Why This Book Exists

This book exists to remind you that while you may feel squeezed in the middle, you are far from powerless. Here, you'll find tools, stories, and strategies to help you:

continued

- Balance family care with your own future.
- Release guilt and set healthy boundaries.
- Build financial stability, even while supporting multiple generations.
- Create a legacy that outlives stress and turns into strength.

You Belong Here

Let this book be your companion in the late nights when you wonder how you'll keep going. Let it be the voice that says:

- You are not alone.
- You are not failing.
- You are enough.

The journey of the Sandwich Generation is heavy, but it's also sacred. And together, we're going to learn how not just to survive it — but to thrive in it.

The Unique Challenges People of Color Face

Being part of the Sandwich Generation is difficult for everyone — but for many people of color, the weight is even heavier. Our experiences are shaped not only by family responsibilities, but also by **cultural expectations** and **historical financial inequities** that make balancing it all uniquely challenging.

Cultural Expectations

In many communities of color, family is not just immediate — **it's extended, interconnected, and collective.** This can be beautiful and grounding, but it also brings heavy expectations:

- **Elders deserve at-home care.** Sending parents to assisted living is often seen as disrespectful or abandonment.
- **The successful one carries the family.** If you've "made it," you're expected to help siblings, cousins, or extended relatives.
- **Sacrifice is honored**. Putting yourself last is often praised as love and loyalty, even when it leads to burnout.

This cultural lens means that saying "no" often feels like betrayal — and guilt becomes a constant companion.

Historical Wealth Gaps

Generational wealth is not equally distributed. Due to systemic racism and exclusion from wealth-building opportunities — such as redlining, job discrimination, and unequal access to credit — many families of color have had fewer assets to pass down.

This creates real financial challenges:

- Parents often enter retirement with limited savings, relying on children for support.
- Homeownership rates are lower, limiting equity transfer between generations.
- Families may face debt cycles that prevent long-term financial stability.

According to Federal Reserve data, the median wealth of Black and Latino families is significantly lower than that of white families — meaning Sandwich Generation caregivers in these communities often carry **responsibility without a safety net.**

Access to Resources

Estate planning, financial advising, and caregiving services often feel out of reach or inaccessible. Families of color may lack:

INTRODUCTION

continued

- Affordable, culturally sensitive financial planners.
- Knowledge about programs like Medicaid, Social Security benefits, or caregiver support funds.
- Legal resources to create wills, trusts, or health care directives.

The result is that too many people end up reinventing the wheel, struggling alone, or losing wealth in probate battles.

The Resilience Factor

And yet, despite these challenges, families of color bring extraordinary **strength and resilience**:

- Strong networks of family and community support.
- Deep traditions of resourcefulness, caregiving, and survival.
- A powerful commitment to lifting up the next generation, even at personal cost.

This resilience is a foundation — but with planning, education, and boundary-setting, it doesn't have to come at the expense of individual well-being.

Key Takeaway

For people of color, the Sandwich Generation journey is not just about family — it's also about **navigating cultural expectations and systemic financial barriers**. Acknowledging these unique challenges is the first step toward breaking cycles and building a future where love and care do not mean sacrifice without security.

Section

BY SECTION

CHAPTER 1
What it Means to Be in the Sandwich Generation

The Invisible Struggle:

If you've ever felt stretched so thin that you wonder how you're still standing, you're not alone. Millions of adults are caught in the middle of **caring for children and supporting aging parents at the same time.**

This is what we call the **Sandwich Generation**. Like the filling between two slices of bread, you're being **pulled in two directions** — emotionally, financially, and physically — as you try to meet the needs of both generations while also trying to care for yourself.

For many in communities of color, this struggle is intensified by **cultural expectations**, limited financial resources, and historical inequities. It can feel like you're carrying **not just a family**, but a legacy, on your back.

This chapter will help you:
- Understand exactly what it means to be in the Sandwich Generation
- Recognize the unique challenges you face
- Identify signs of stress and burnout early
- Begin to see that you can thrive with the right tools and mindset

Who Is the Sandwich Generation?

The term "Sandwich Generation" was first used in the 1980s by social worker Dorothy Miller. It describes adults, typically between ages **35 and 59**, who are **raising young or teenage children while simultaneously caring for aging parents.**

But over time, this definition has expanded. Today, the Sandwich Generation includes:
- Adults supporting **college-aged or financially dependent adult children**

CHAPTER 1
What it Means to Be in the Sandwich Generation

- People providing **care or financial support to grandparents, siblings, or extended family**
- Caregivers who may not have kids of their own but are the **primary support for elderly relatives**

Essentially, if you're stuck between the needs of two or more generations, you're part of this group.

A Day in the Life of the "Middle"

Imagine this:
You start your morning packing lunches for your kids before rushing to a doctor's appointment with your mom, who recently had knee surgery. On your lunch break, you're on the phone with your teenage daughter's school about her college applications. By evening, you're paying bills — not just yours, but your father's — while trying to figure out how to contribute to your retirement account this month.

By the end of the day, you're completely drained, yet still feeling guilty for not doing enough.

This is the everyday reality of being in the Sandwich Generation.

CHAPTER 1
What it Means to Be in the Sandwich Generation

Why This Hits Communities of Color Harder

For African American, Latino, and other communities of color, being in the Sandwich Generation comes with **unique challenges:**

1. Cultural Expectations of Care

Many cultures emphasize **family loyalty and multigenerational living,** which can be beautiful and grounding. But it can also mean:

- Feeling **obligated** to financially support parents or siblings, even when it strains your own budget.
- Struggling to set boundaries without being seen as disrespectful or selfish.
- Carrying a "firstborn" or "successful child" burden where others expect you to fix everything.

2. Historical Wealth Gaps

Due to systemic barriers, many families of color haven't had the same opportunities to build wealth. This often leads to:

- Parents entering retirement without enough savings, needing your support.
- Limited family inheritance or assets to pass down.
- A cycle where each generation has to **start over financially.**

Statistic: According to a 2023 Federal Reserve report, the median wealth of Black families is about **one-sixth** that of white families. This directly impacts how caregiving and financial responsibilities are shared.

3. Lack of Accessible Resources

- Many families don't have **financial planners**, legal advisors, or healthcare advocates who understand their specific situations.
- Government programs can be **confusing** or **hard to access** without guidance.
- This leaves caregivers feeling isolated and overwhelmed.

The Emotional Toll: Signs of Caregiver Burnout

Being sandwiched between two generations doesn't just drain your wallet — it can also drain your **emotional and physical energy.**

CHAPTER 1
What it Means to Be in the Sandwich Generation

Here are some common warning signs of burnout:

- **Exhaustion:** Always tired, no matter how much you rest
- **Irritability:** Snapping at loved ones over small things
- **Guilt:** Feeling like you're never doing enough for anyone
- **Neglected health:** Skipping your own doctor appointments or self-care
- **Isolation:** Withdrawing from friends and activities you once enjoyed
- **Financial stress:** Constant worry about bills and future expenses

If you see yourself in this list, it's not a personal failure — it's a sign that you're carrying **too much alone**, and it's time to seek support.

Why Naming It Matters

You might wonder, "Why does it even matter that there's a name for this?"

When you can **name your struggle**, you can **begin to address it.**

Recognizing yourself as part of the Sandwich Generation validates your experience and helps you realize:

- You're **not alone** — millions of others are in similar situations.
- There are **strategies and resources** created specifically for people like you.
- You can start building a plan to balance caregiving, finances, and your future.

Think of it like this: Naming your challenge is the first step toward taking back control of your life.

KEY TAKEAWAY

Being in the Sandwich Generation is both a privilege and a challenge. You have the opportunity to shape the lives of those you love most — your children and your parents — while building a legacy of care, stability, and resilience.
But you can't do it all alone, and you don't have to.

The rest of this book will help you **move from surviving to thriving** by:

- Setting clear boundaries
- Creating financial strategies for stability
- Learning to care for yourself as much as you care for others
- Building a legacy that lasts for generations

"I love my parents. I love my kids. But some days, I feel like there's nothing left for me."
– A voice from the middle

Reflection Questions

- [ ] What caregiving responsibilities do you currently have?

  _____

- [ ] Which relationships feel most draining right now — and why?

  _____

- [ ] Where are you currently struggling the most: emotionally, financially, or physically?

  _____

- [ ] What would a balanced, thriving life look like for you?

  _____

- [ ] _____

- [ ] _____

- [ ] _____

- [ ] _____

REFLECTION QUESTIONS FOR THE SANDWICH GENERATION

Chapter

2

CHAPTER 2
Cultural Expectations and Family Pressure

The Unspoken Rules

Every culture carries unspoken rules about family. For many people of color, those rules are deeply rooted in **love, loyalty, and survival**. We are taught from childhood that family comes first, and that we owe our parents and elders respect, support, and gratitude.

But what happens when those expectations collide with your own needs, goals, and limits?

This chapter explores how cultural norms shape the Sandwich Generation experience, and how you can navigate them with both **honor and boundaries.**

The Weight of Cultural Duty

In many communities of color, there are common expectations:

- **Elders deserve care at home**. Sending parents to nursing facilities is often seen as abandonment.
- **The eldest carries the load**. Firstborn children, especially daughters, are expected to shoulder the most responsibility.
- **Success means giving back**. If you've "made it" financially, it's assumed you'll support not just your parents but also siblings and extended family.
- **Sacrifice is honorable**. Struggling for family is often praised, even if it leads to burnout.

These values come from a place of love and resilience — but when left unchecked, they can create crushing **pressure and guilt.**

How Family Pressure Shows Up

CHAPTER 2
Cultural Expectations and Family Pressure

Family pressure doesn't always sound like yelling or demands. Sometimes it's subtle — a sigh, a story about "what so-and-so's daughter did," or even silence that makes you feel like you've fallen short.

Here are a few ways it may show up:

- **Guilt trips:** "After everything I've done for you, this is how you repay me?"
- **Comparison:** "Your cousin helps her mom every week — why can't you?"
- **Financial expectations:** Assumptions that you'll cover bills, weddings, or emergencies.
- **Invisible labor:** Expecting you to organize, plan, or coordinate family matters, even if others could help.

Over time, these pressures can lead to **resentment, financial instability, and emotional burnout.**

The Double-Edged Sword of Respect

Respect for parents and elders is sacred. It's a foundation of many cultures. But respect should not mean **self-erasure.**

Healthy respect says:

- "I honor you, but I cannot destroy myself to help you."
- "I love you, but I need to set limits."
- "I will support you, but I also must build my own future."

When respect turns into obligation without boundaries, it becomes a **burden instead of a blessing.**

15

CHAPTER 2
Cultural Expectations and Family Pressure

Real Stories from the Middle

- **Marisol, 47, Latina**: "When my mom got sick, my brothers said, 'You're the daughter, you should handle it.' I was working full-time and raising kids. I finally realized I couldn't do it all. It was painful to say no, but necessary."
- **Derrick, 52, African American**: "I send money to my parents every month. I don't mind, but when my siblings started depending on me too, I felt trapped. It took me years to set boundaries without feeling like a bad son."

These are not isolated stories — they are lived realities for millions.

How to Honor Tradition and Protect Yourself

You don't have to reject your culture or disrespect your family to create balance. You can do both — honor and protect.

1. Redefine What Support Looks Like

Support doesn't always mean money or constant time. It can mean:

- Helping parents access benefits or healthcare services
- Sharing caregiving responsibilities with siblings
- Offering emotional support instead of financial support

2. Communicate with Love

Instead of saying "I can't," try:

- "I love you, and here's what I can do."
- "I want to help, but I also need to take care of my future. Let's find a solution together."

3. Involve the Whole Family

Don't let caregiving fall on one person. Call family meetings. Divide tasks based on skills, not just tradition.

4. Release the Guilt

Remember: Taking care of yourself is also taking care of your family. If you burn out, you won't be able to help anyone.

KEY TAKEAWAY

Cultural expectations are powerful, but they don't have to control you. You can respect your roots while also creating **new, healthier traditions** — ones where love does not equal self-sacrifice, and where caregiving is a shared responsibility.

This balance is the heart of surviving — and thriving — in the Sandwich Generation.

"In our family, you don't put your parents in a home. You take care of them — no matter what."

Tanya is a single mom raising a teenage daughter while also caring for her 72-year-old mother who moved in after a health scare. She contributes to her daughter's 529 college plan, but her mother's medical expenses often eat into her budget. Tanya's breakthrough came when she created a multi-generational budget where everyone contributed what they could — even her daughter added small amounts from a part-time job.

Lesson: Small, consistent contributions add up, and involving the whole family in financial transparency eases pressure.

📖 **Case Study:** Marcus, 49, Georgia

Marcus was offered a job promotion that required relocation, but turning it down felt like the only option. His parents rely on him for daily care, and his teenage sons are deeply rooted in their school community. While he sometimes feels stuck, Marcus reframed his choice as an investment in family stability rather than a lost career opportunity.

Lesson: Not every sacrifice is a setback — sometimes stability is the best legacy.

📖 **Case Study:** Keisha, 42, Illinois

Growing up, Keisha never heard her parents talk about money. Now, as a caregiver for her father and raising two children, she realized silence was part of the cycle. She began hosting monthly family money talks over Sunday dinner. At first, it was uncomfortable, but eventually, her kids and father began opening up about their needs, fears, and goals.

Lesson: Talking about money openly across generations can break cycles of secrecy and build shared responsibility.

Mini Stories

18

📖 **Case Study:** Darnell, 46, Texas

Darnell has 20 years of service as a federal employee but withdrew from his retirement account years ago to cover a crisis for his brother. Now, with three kids and his in-laws moving in, he felt far behind. By maxing out his catch-up contributions in his TSP and cutting discretionary expenses as a family, he's slowly rebuilding.

Lesson: It's never too late to catch up on retirement savings with focused planning and family buy-in.

📖 **Case Study:** Angela, 51, California

Angela cares for her elderly aunt while raising her college-aged son. She used to feel guilty she couldn't provide lavish financial support. Instead, she started emphasizing emotional support and shared skills — teaching her son budgeting and involving her aunt in family decisions.

Lesson: Legacy isn't only financial — it's also about teaching resilience, values, and practical life skills.

Mini Stories

Reflection Questions

☐ What family expectations are weighing on me right now?

☐ Which of these expectations are cultural traditions I value – and which feel harmful?

☐ How can I reframe "support" in a way that honors family but also protects me?

☐ Where do I need to set boundaries, and how can I communicate them respectfully?

☐

☐

☐

☐

REFLECTION QUESTIONS FOR THE SANDWICH GENERATION

Kids

Parents

Me

CHAPTER 3
Retirement Planning When You're Supporting Everyone Else

The Retirement Catch-22

One of the hardest realities of the Sandwich Generation is that while you're busy supporting everyone else, your **own retirement planning often falls behind.**

You're likely helping with:

- Kids' school or college costs
- Monthly bills for parents or relatives
- Emergencies that pop up when someone calls and says, "Can you help me out this month?"

But here's the truth: **if you don't prioritize your retirement, you may end up needing the very support you're giving now.**

This chapter is about learning how to **balance today's responsibilities with tomorrow's security.**

Why Retirement Planning Gets Delayed

Many in the Sandwich Generation delay retirement saving for three main reasons:

1. **Cultural Pressure**
   It feels selfish to put money aside for yourself when others have immediate needs.
2. **Financial Gaps**
   With the rising costs of childcare, healthcare, and housing, retirement feels like a "someday" priority.
3. **Emotional Guilt**
   You may think: *"If I don't help my parents now, what does that say about me as a child?"*
   Or: *"If I don't give my kids the best, I'm failing them."*

The result? You risk shortchanging your future.

The Golden Rule: Pay Yourself First

It may sound harsh, but the most loving thing you can do for your family is to secure your own financial future.

Think of it like being on an airplane: **you must put your oxygen mask on first.** If you run out of air, you can't help anyone else.

Practical steps:
- Treat retirement savings like a **non-negotiable bill**.
- Automate contributions so you don't "accidentally" spend the money.
- Even small amounts add up over time.

Catch-Up Strategies for Midlife Savers

If you feel behind, you're not alone — and it's not too late. Here are proven strategies:

1. Maximize Workplace Accounts
- If you have access to a **401(k) or TSP (for federal employees)**, take advantage of **catch-up contributions** (available once you're 50).
- Always contribute at least enough to get the full employer match — it's free money.

2. Consider Roth vs. Traditional
- **Traditional accounts** lower your taxable income now but are taxed later.
- **Roth accounts** are taxed now, but withdrawals in retirement are tax-free.
- If you expect your tax bracket to be higher in retirement, a Roth may benefit you more.

3. Open an IRA

Even if you're maxing out your work plan, you can also contribute to an **IRA (Individual Retirement Account)** for additional tax advantages.

4. Downsize or Adjust Lifestyle

- Consider downsizing your home once kids are grown.
- Cut unnecessary subscriptions or expenses and redirect that money into retirement.

Balancing Family Support with Retirement

Here's how to support family *without sabotaging yourself*:

For Kids:

- Set clear boundaries about what you will cover (e.g., partial college tuition, not full).
- Encourage scholarships, grants, or part-time work.
- Teach them financial literacy early so they aren't dependent on you long-term.

For Parents:

- Help them access government programs (Medicare, Medicaid, Social Security).
- Share costs with siblings instead of carrying it all.
- Explore community and nonprofit resources that reduce expenses.

Legacy Thinking: Breaking the Cycle

Many of us in the Sandwich Generation are determined to **break cycles of financial struggle**. By planning your retirement now, you not only protect yourself — you also give your kids a roadmap.

Imagine this: instead of your children supporting you one day, you're able to **leave them a legacy** — not just financially, but in wisdom and stability.

Quick Financial Action Plan

1. Calculate your retirement number (what you'll need monthly in retirement).
2. Check your current savings rate against that number.
3. Increase contributions by even 1–2% each year.
4. Meet with a financial planner — ideally one who understands cultural family obligations.
5. Revisit your plan annually.

KEY TAKEAWAY

Retirement planning is not selfish. It's an act of **love and protection**. By prioritizing your own financial health, you ensure that your children and parents don't face even greater burdens down the road.

You can care for your family today **and** secure your future tomorrow — but it starts with putting your oxygen mask on first.

"I feel guilty saving for myself when my parents need help and my kids still depend on me. But I also don't want to be a burden when I'm older."

Reflection Questions

☐ How much am I currently saving for retirement each month?

_____

☐ Am I putting family needs ahead of my future security? Where is that hurting me most?

_____

☐ What small change could I make this month to increase my retirement savings?

_____

☐ What legacy do I want to leave for my children – financial, emotional, and cultural?

_____

☐ _____

☐ _____

☐ _____

☐ _____

REFLECTION
QUESTIONS
FOR THE
SANDWICH
GENERATION

Chapter

— 4 —

CHAPTER 4
Smart Money Moves for Multi-Generational Households

The Juggling Act

Living in or supporting a **multi-generational household** is both rewarding and challenging. There's community, shared love, and a sense of cultural continuity. But financially? It can feel like trying to stretch one blanket over too many people.

This chapter will show you how to **regain control of your household finances**, even when multiple generations rely on you.

Why Multi-Generational Finances Are Tricky

Unlike a single-income or nuclear-family budget, multi-generational finances often involve:

- **Multiple incomes** coming in, but not always evenly shared.
- **Different expenses** for children, parents, and sometimes even siblings.
- **Unequal expectations** — one person may feel responsible for more than their fair share.
- **Blurry boundaries** around who pays for what.

Without a plan, money in these households can quickly disappear without anyone knowing where it went.

Step 1: Create a Transparent Household Budget

The first step is clarity. Write down **all income streams and all expenses** in one place.

Categories to include:

- Mortgage or rent
- Utilities (electric, water, internet, phone)

- Groceries
- Transportation (gas, insurance, car payments)
- Medical/healthcare expenses
- Debt payments (student loans, credit cards)
- Children's expenses (school, activities, college savings)
- Elder care expenses (medications, in-home care, support services)
- Retirement and savings contributions

Pro Tip: Use a shared Google Sheet or budgeting app that everyone contributing can see. This increases accountability and reduces hidden burdens.

Step 2: Define Who Pays What

Money stress often comes from unclear expectations.

- If multiple adults live in the same household, **divide expenses fairly** — not necessarily equally.
- For example: a parent living with you may contribute to groceries or utilities, while you cover housing.
- Teenagers or young adult children living at home can contribute with part-time income.

Remember: **contribution builds responsibility**. Allowing everyone to pitch in fosters fairness and reduces resentment.

Step 3: Build an Emergency Fund for the Whole Family

Emergencies are guaranteed in multi-generational households. Whether it's a medical bill, job loss, or unexpected car repair, having a shared **family emergency fund** can save you from high-interest debt.

- Start with a goal of **$1,000 minimum**, then build toward **3–6 months of expenses.**
- Keep this money separate from checking so it's not accidentally spent.

Step 4: Protect Against Debt Traps

When you're caring for multiple people, it's tempting to rely on credit cards or loans. But debt can quickly snowball.

- Prioritize paying off **high-interest debt first** (like credit cards).
- Avoid co-signing loans for relatives unless you can afford to take on the debt yourself.
- If family members ask for money regularly, consider setting a **monthly "helping fund"** so you're giving within limits, not at the expense of your retirement.

Step 5: Make Savings Automatic

Even with family responsibilities, you can't afford to skip saving.

- Automate contributions to retirement accounts (401k, TSP, IRA).
- Create a **separate savings account** for children's education or future goals.
- Teach your kids to save a portion of any money they receive — birthdays, allowance, jobs.

Step 6: Open Communication

The hardest part isn't the math — it's the conversations. Money is emotional, and in families, it can be taboo. But silence breeds resentment.

Tips for smoother talks:

- Schedule monthly "family money check-ins."
- Be honest about your limits: "Here's what I can contribute. Beyond that, it hurts my stability."
- Frame conversations around shared goals — not just bills, but dreams (retirement security, kids' future, parents' dignity).

KEY TAKEAWAY

Multi-generational households work best when finances are **transparent, shared, and balanced**. You can't do it all alone, and you shouldn't have to. With clarity, boundaries, and open communication, your family can thrive — not just survive — together.

"It feels like my paycheck comes in and goes right back out between kids, parents, and bills, where does it all go?"

Reflection Questions

- [ ] Do I have a clear picture of all household income and expenses?

- [ ] Who contributes what in my household – and does it feel fair?

- [ ] What financial boundaries do I need to set to protect myself and my future?

- [ ] How can I start family money conversations in a loving but firm way?

- [ ]

- [ ]

- [ ]

- [ ]

REFLECTION QUESTIONS FOR THE SANDWICH GENERATION

Chapter

5

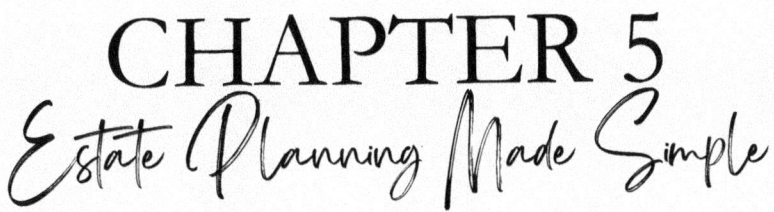

The Gift of Planning

Estate planning is one of the most avoided conversations in families — yet it's also one of the most loving things you can do. Too many families of color have lost wealth, property, and even relationships because plans weren't made in advance.

The truth is, estate planning is not just for the wealthy. It's for **anyone who cares about protecting their loved ones, avoiding conflict, and passing on stability instead of struggle.**

Why Estate Planning Matters

Without a plan:
- The state decides how your assets are divided (through probate court).
- Family members may argue, sometimes permanently damaging relationships.
- Your children or dependents may not be cared for as you would want.

With a plan:
- You choose who inherits what.
- You reduce stress and confusion for your loved ones.
- You create a legacy of intention and protection.

Key Tools for Estate Planning

Estate planning doesn't have to be complicated. Here are the essentials:

CHAPTER 5
Estate Planning Made Simple

1. A Will
- A legal document that outlines who will receive your assets after your death.
- Allows you to name guardians for minor children.
- Without one, your estate will be divided according to state law.

2. A Trust
- A legal arrangement where your assets are held for your beneficiaries.
- Helps your family avoid probate (a long, public, and expensive process).
- Can be used to protect property and pass down assets smoothly.

3. Power of Attorney
- Gives someone the legal right to handle your finances if you can't.
- Ensures bills are paid and decisions are made in your best interest.

4. Healthcare Proxy / Advance Directive
- Names someone to make medical decisions for you if you're unable.
- Clarifies your wishes around life support, treatments, and end-of-life care.

5. Beneficiary Designations
- Many accounts (retirement, life insurance, bank accounts) allow you to name beneficiaries directly.
- These override your will — so it's critical to keep them updated.

Why Many Families Avoid It

In our communities, estate planning is often delayed because:

- Talking about death feels uncomfortable or disrespectful.
- There's a belief that "I don't have enough to need a will."
- Lack of access to affordable legal services.

But avoiding it doesn't protect your family — it **leaves them vulnerable.**

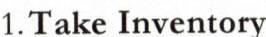

CHAPTER 5
Estate Planning Made Simple

Steps to Get Started

1. **Take Inventory**
   - List all your assets: home, car, bank accounts, retirement accounts, life insurance, and valuable items.
   - List your debts: mortgage, loans, credit cards.
2. **Decide Who Gets What**
   - Be specific to avoid disputes.
   - Consider both financial assets and sentimental items.
3. **Name Guardians and Executors**
   - Choose someone trustworthy to handle your estate.
   - Make sure they know your wishes.
4. **Work With a Professional**
   - Consider meeting with an estate planning attorney.
   - For lower-cost options, check nonprofit legal clinics or online services.
5. **Communicate With Your Family**
   - Share your plan openly to reduce future conflict.
   - Explain your decisions to avoid surprises later.

Breaking Generational Cycles

Estate planning is about more than money — it's about **empowerment and generational stability.** For too long, families of color have lost homes, land, and savings because no plan was in place.

By creating a will or trust, you're making sure your family doesn't have to start from scratch. You're building a bridge toward generational wealth and security.

CHAPTER 5
Estate Planning Made Simple

KEY TAKEAWAY

Estate planning isn't about preparing for death — it's about **protecting life, love, and legacy**. Creating a plan today is one of the greatest gifts you can leave for tomorrow.

"I don't want to think about death, but I also don't want my family fighting or struggling when I'm gone."

Reflection Questions

- ☐ Do I currently have a will, trust, or power of attorney in place? _____
- ☐ What assets do I want to pass down – and to whom? _____
- ☐ Who in my life do I trust to carry out my wishes? _____
- ☐ What conversations do I need to have with my family about these decisions? _____
- ☐ _____
- ☐ _____
- ☐ _____
- ☐ _____

REFLECTION QUESTIONS FOR THE SANDWICH GENERATION

Chapter

6

CHAPTER 6
Supporting Your Kids Without Going Broke

As parents, especially within communities of color, we often feel an immense responsibility to set our children up for success. Many of us were raised with limited resources, and now that we've reached a certain level of stability, we want our kids to have a better life than we did.

But here's the hard truth: **over-giving can sabotage your retirement and their growth.**

Your goal is to raise children who are capable, resilient, and financially independent — not to sacrifice your future so they can have the latest sneakers or graduate debt-free while you work until you're 80.

The Mindset Shift: Teaching Independence vs. Providing Comfort

It's natural to want to make your kids' path easier. But ask yourself:

* Am I teaching my children how to earn and manage money, or just giving them what they ask for?
* Am I funding their lifestyle at the expense of my retirement security?
* Will they be able to thrive without me financially?

The earlier you shift from **provider** to **coach**, the more successful both you and your kids will be.

Smart Strategies for Supporting Kids

1. Establish Clear Financial Boundaries

* Decide exactly what you will and will not pay for.
  * Example: "We'll help with 50% of college costs, but you'll need scholarships or part-time work to cover the rest."

- Put these agreements in writing — even a simple family contract can prevent misunderstandings.

2. Teach Them About Money Early

- Start conversations about budgeting, credit, and saving in middle school or earlier.
- Encourage teens to get summer or part-time jobs.
- Share real numbers — let them see what bills actually cost so they understand household expenses.

3. Plan for College Without Sacrificing Retirement

- Consider a **529 savings plan** or **Coverdell ESA** if you can save ahead.
- Have honest conversations about affordable school choices.
- Remember: There are loans for college, **but no loans for retirement**.

Prioritizing Needs Over Wants

Kids today are surrounded by messages equating love with material things. But true support is ensuring their needs are met and their future is stable. Ask yourself: Is this expense a true need or a temporary want? Setting limits teaches resilience and prepares them for adulthood.

Quick Win: The Allowance that Teaches

Instead of giving kids a weekly allowance just for existing, tie money to tasks or achievements.

- 30% goes to spending
- 30% goes to saving
- 30% goes to investing or long-term goals
- 10% goes to giving back

This simple formula builds lifelong habits and connects them to values beyond consumerism.

KEY TAKEAWAY

Supporting your kids without going broke is about balance. It's about showing them that financial health is a family affair, and that sometimes saying "no" now ensures stability later. Remember — their future includes you. Protecting your retirement and financial health is one of the greatest gifts you can give your children.

"We want to give our kids everything we never had. But sometimes, in doing so, we risk giving them a future of dependency rather than independence."

Reflection Questions

☐ What values about money do I want my children to learn from me?

☐ Where am I over-extending myself financially in ways that don't align with my family's real needs or goals?

☐ How can I include my children in financial decision-making that affects them?

☐ What does 'enough' look like for our family right now?

☐

☐

☐

☐

REFLECTION QUESTIONS FOR THE SANDWICH GENERATION

43

Chapter

7

CHAPTER 7
Caring for Aging Parents with Grace and Boundaries

Caring for aging parents is one of the greatest honors — and one of the greatest stressors — you may ever experience. For many of us, there's a cultural expectation to step in without question, especially if you're the eldest or the most financially stable sibling.

But caregiving without clear boundaries can lead to **burnout, resentment, and financial strain**. The key is to approach this season with both **love and strategy**.

The Emotional Side of Caregiving

Watching your parents decline in health or independence is emotionally heavy. It often brings:

- Guilt — "Am I doing enough?"
- Pressure — from siblings or extended family
- Fear — about costs, decisions, and the future

The first step to protecting yourself is **acknowledging your feelings are valid**. You cannot pour from an empty cup.

Having Hard Conversations

Talking to parents about their future care and finances is tough but necessary.
Here's a framework to make it easier:

1. Choose the Right Time

- Pick a calm moment, not during a health crisis or family argument.
- Let them know the conversation is coming: "I'd like to talk about how we can plan together for the future."

2. Lead with Love and Respect

- Start by affirming their independence and dignity.
  - Example: "I want to make sure your wishes are honored and you have the best care possible."

3. Cover These Essential Topics:

- **Medical care** — preferred doctors, treatments, and emergency plans
- **Living arrangements** — staying home, assisted living, moving in with family
- **Financials** — income, debts, insurance, and assets
- **Legal documents** — will, power of attorney, health care proxy

When Siblings Disagree

Family disagreements over caregiving are common.
To avoid tension:

- Divide responsibilities based on strengths (not just location).
  - Example: One sibling handles finances, another coordinates doctor visits.
- Consider **family meetings** every few months to keep communication open.
- If needed, bring in a neutral third party like a financial planner or eldercare mediator.

Preventing Caregiver Burnout

Caring for parents can consume every ounce of your energy if you let it.
Protect yourself with these strategies:

CHAPTER 7
Caring for Aging Parents with Grace and Boundaries

- **Set limits** on how much time you can realistically give each week.
- **Accept help** — whether from siblings, friends, or professional caregivers.
- **Prioritize self-care** like exercise, rest, and therapy.
- **Join a support group** — online or in person — to connect with others going through the same challenges.

Remember: Your parents need you at your best, not your most exhausted.

Quick Resource: Caregiving Conversation Starter

- "Mom, Dad, I want to make sure I understand your wishes as you get older."
- "How do you envision your care in the future?"
- "Have you made any plans for your finances or living situation as you age?"
- "What would give you the most peace of mind?"

Closing Reflection for Section 3

Balancing care for children and parents is an act of love — but it's also a tremendous responsibility. The goal isn't perfection or self-sacrifice. It's about **creating sustainable systems** so you can care for others without losing yourself.

Take it one conversation, one boundary, and one decision at a time.

"You can love your parents deeply and still protect your mental health, your finances, and your future."

Reflection Questions

REFLECTION QUESTIONS FOR THE SANDWICH GENERATION

☐ How do I define "grace" in my caregiving journey? _____

☐ Where do I need to set clearer boundaries to protect my well-being? _____

☐ In what ways do cultural or family expectations influence how I care for my parents? ____

☐ What kind of support do I need – emotionally, financially, or practically – to sustain this role long term? _____

☐ _____

☐ _____

☐ _____

☐ _____

BREAKING GENERATIONAL CYCLES

Chapter

8

CHAPTER 8
Breaking Generational Cycles

From Survival to Legacy

Many of us in the Sandwich Generation carry two truths at once:

1. Gratitude for the sacrifices our parents and grandparents made.
2. A desire to give our children more opportunities than we had.

This tension is the heart of **breaking generational cycles**. It means choosing to end patterns of struggle, instability, or silence — and replacing them with knowledge, stability, and empowerment.

The Cycles We Inherit

Generational cycles don't happen by accident. They are passed down through lived experiences, both good and bad. Some common ones in communities of color include:

- **Financial instability**: Limited savings, reliance on debt, lack of generational wealth.
- **Silence about money**: Parents avoiding financial conversations, leaving children unprepared.
- **Caregiver burnout**: Each generation taking on heavy burdens without a plan.
- **Missed opportunities**: Not accessing resources like retirement accounts, homeownership programs, or scholarships due to lack of knowledge.

Breaking these cycles doesn't mean blaming our elders — it means **acknowledging the challenges and choosing a different path forward.**

Why It Matters

Without intentional change, the same struggles will repeat.

Children may inherit:
- Debt instead of wealth.
- Confusion instead of financial literacy.
- Pressure instead of planning.

Breaking cycles ensures the next generation has **tools, confidence, and security,** so they aren't forced to start over from zero.

Step 1: Teach Financial Literacy Early

Money should not be a taboo subject. Teach children:

- How to budget and save.
- The importance of credit and how to manage it wisely.
- How to invest for the future.
- That wealth isn't just money — it's freedom, choices, and peace of mind.

Tip: Start small. Even sharing the family budget or explaining how bills work gives kids real-world understanding.

Step 2: Model Boundaries

Children learn not only from what we say, but from what we do.

- When you set limits with family members, you show your children that boundaries are healthy.
- When you prioritize saving for retirement, you teach them that planning matters.

Modeling responsible financial behavior is one of the most powerful legacies you can leave.

Step 3: Document and Share Knowledge

One reason cycles repeat is that **knowledge gets lost**.

- Write down your financial plan, account information, and important documents.
- Create a **"family playbook"** that includes emergency contacts, insurance info, and estate planning details. (You can download my Sh*t you should know if I die guide.)
- Share this openly so your children aren't left in the dark.

Step 4: Build Generational Wealth

Even if you start small, every step matters:

- Buy **life insurance** (so your family inherits stability, not debt).
- Invest consistently, even in modest amounts.
- Prioritize homeownership or other appreciating assets if possible.
- Use estate planning tools (like wills and trusts) to make wealth transfer smooth.

Step 5: Redefine Legacy

Legacy is more than money. It's also about:

- Passing down values like resilience, compassion, and community.
- Creating traditions that strengthen identity.
- Leaving behind stories of perseverance and triumph, so the next generation knows where they come from.

KEY TAKEAWAY

Breaking generational cycles is not about rejecting the past — it's about **building on it**. Your parents and grandparents may not have had the tools, but you do. By making intentional choices today, you're planting seeds of security, freedom, and dignity for generations to come.

"My parents did the best they could with what they had. But I want my children to start from a stronger place than I did."

Reflection Questions

☐ What cycles did I inherit from my family that I don't want to repeat?

☐ What positive values and lessons do I want to carry forward?

☐ How can I start teaching financial literacy to my children or younger relatives today?

☐ What steps can I take in the next 12 months to begin building generational wealth?

☐

☐

☐

☐

REFLECTION QUESTIONS FOR THE SANDWICH GENERATION

Chapter

9

Family
Legacy

CHAPTER 9
Designing Your Legacy Plan

From Dreams to Blueprint

Legacy doesn't happen by chance — it happens by design. Too often, families leave behind confusion, conflict, or debt instead of stability. Designing your legacy means creating a clear, intentional plan that blends **financial security, family traditions, and personal values.**

This chapter gives you a framework to design a legacy plan that ensures your loved ones inherit not just money, but also **clarity, dignity, and direction.**

Step 1: Define What Legacy Means to You

Legacy is more than assets. It's about **what you want to be remembered** for. Ask yourself:

- What values do I want to pass on (faith, education, resilience, generosity)?
- What stories or lessons do I want my children and grandchildren to know?
- What kind of financial or practical foundation do I want to leave behind?

This is your **why**, and it guides everything else.

Step 2: Build Your Family Financial Playbook

A family financial playbook is a simple document that lays out your household's financial blueprint. It should include:

- **Asset inventory:** Property, bank accounts, retirement accounts, insurance policies.
- **Debt list**: Loans, mortgages, credit cards, medical bills.
- **Important contacts**: Lawyer, financial planner, insurance agent, executor.
- **Instructions**: Who gets what, and how to access accounts.

Tip: Keep it simple, updated, and in a secure but accessible place.

Step 3: Put the Right Tools in Place

To protect your legacy, formalize it with legal and financial tools:

- **Will**: Clearly state how assets should be divided.
- **Trust**: Avoid probate and protect assets for children.
- **Insurance**: Life insurance ensures your family inherits stability, not debt.
- **Beneficiaries**: Keep designations up to date on retirement accounts and policies.
- **Letters to Loved Ones**: Beyond legal papers, write personal letters explaining your decisions, hopes, and values.

Step 4: Create Traditions That Outlive You

Your legacy is also cultural and emotional. Design intentional traditions that strengthen family bonds:

- Family reunions or holiday rituals.
- Storytelling nights where elders share history.
- A scholarship fund for younger generations.
- A family volunteering day or charitable tradition.

These intangible legacies are just as powerful as financial ones.

Step 5: Communicate Your Plan

A legacy plan works best when your family understands it.

- Call a **family meeting** to explain your wishes.
- Be transparent about what you can and cannot provide.
- Answer questions while you're here, so confusion doesn't happen when you're gone.

Clear communication prevents conflict and ensures your plan is respected.

KEY TAKEAWAY

Designing your legacy is an act of **love, clarity, and leadership**. By putting your intentions into action, you create a future where your family is not burdened with confusion, but blessed with stability and purpose.

Legacy is not just what you leave. It's how you live today to shape tomorrow.

"A legacy is not what you leave behind by accident. It's what you build with intention."

Reflection Questions

☐ What values and lessons do I want to pass down beyond money?

_____

☐ Do I have a complete list of my assets, debts, and beneficiaries?

_____

☐ What traditions can I create now that will carry on for future generations?

_____

☐ Who in my family should know the details of my plan – and how will I share it?

_____

☐ _____

☐ _____

☐ _____

☐ _____

THE SANDWICH GENERATION WORKSHEETS

WORKBOOKS

Practical Tools for Balancing Kids, Parents, and Yourself

Workbook Introduction

- **Purpose:**
- This workbook is your space to take action on the strategies in Chapters 6 and 7. Use it to plan conversations, set boundaries, and get clarity on how to care for your loved ones without losing yourself.

- **How to Use It:**
  - Print it or fill it out digitally on a tablet or computer.
  - Complete one worksheet at a time — don't overwhelm yourself.
  - Revisit regularly as situations change.

61

WORKBOOKS

Worksheet 1: Family Financial Boundaries Checklist

Goal: Define what you will and won't pay for so everyone is clear.

Category	We Will Pay For	We Will Not Pay For	Notes/Exceptions
College tuition	Example: First 2 years at community college	Out-of-State tuition + housing	Child must maintain GPA of 3.0 or higher
Housing (after 18)	Up to 6 months rent if working	Full rent after 6 months	
Car expenses	Car insurance only	Car payment and repairs	
Cell phone	Family plan until age 21	New phone upgrades every year	
Extracurriculars	High School sports fees	Summer camps and expensive trips	
Tip: Print one for each child and keep it visible for reference.			

Worksheet 2: Teen & Young Adult Financial Independence Tracker

Caring for Aging Parents with Grace and Boundaries

Skill/Task	Target Age	Completed? (✓)	Notes
Knows how to budget income	15-16		
Opens and manages a bank account	16-18		
Understands how credit works	16-18		
Files first tax return	17-19		
Knows how to grocery shop & meal plan	15-18		
Can set financial goals	18+		
Goal: By age 21, your child should check off at least 80% of this list.			

WORKBOOKS

Worksheet 3: Caregiving Conversation Planner

Prepare for hard talks with your parents.

Topic	Key Questions to Ask	Notes/Their Answers
Health care preferences	"How do you want to be cared for if your health declines?"	
Living arrangements	"Would you prefer to stay at home, live with family, or move to assisted living?"	
Finances	"Do you have savings, insurance, or pensions to help with costs?"	
Legal documents	"Have you created a will or power of attorney?"	
End-of-life wishes	"What are your spiritual or personal wishes we should honor?"	

Worksheet 4: Caregiving Roles & Responsibilities Map

Prevent family conflict by clearly defining who does what.

Task	Primary Person Responsible	Backup / Support	Notes
Doctor appointments			
Medication management			
Transportation			
Bill payments / finances			
Meal prep & groceries			
Home maintenance			
Emotional support visits			

WORKBOOKS

Worksheet 5: Caregiver Burnout Self-Check

Use this regularly to monitor your stress levels.

For each statement, rate yourself **1 (Strongly Disagree)** to **5 (Strongly Agree)**:

Statement	Score (1-5)
I often feel physically exhausted	
I feel resentment toward family members about caregiving.	
I frequently lose sleep worrying about my parents or kids.	
I don't have time for myself or my hobbies.	
My health has declined since becoming a caregiver.	
I avoid conversations because I feel overwhelmed.	
Totals	

Scoring:

- **6–12**: You're managing well.
- **13–20**: Watch for warning signs — time to delegate or ask for help.
- **21–30**: High risk of burnout — take immediate action to protect your well-being.

Worksheet 6: Support System Map

Identify your caregiving network.

Category	People or Resources	Contact Info	Notes
Family members			
Friends & neighbors			
Paid caregivers / nurses			
Community organizations			
Support Groups (online/in-person			
Medical professionals			

WORKBOOKS

Worksheet 7: Multi-Generational Household Budget Template

This template is designed to help multi-generational households track income and expenses across multiple family members. Use it to plan, coordinate, and create financial transparency in your home.

Category	Monthly Budget	Actual Spent	Notes
Household Income (combined)			
- Parent 1 Income			
- Parent 2 Income			
- Other Adult Income (grandparent/relative)			
Housing (rent/mortgage)			
Utilities (electric, water, gas, internet)			
Groceries & Household Supplies			
Transportation (car, gas, insurance)			
Healthcare (insurance, ou-of-pocket)			
Childcare & Education			
Eldercare Expenses			
Debt Payments (credit, loans)			
Savings & Investments			
Emergency Fund			
Entertainment & Family Activities			
Other Shared Expenses			
Total			

Worksheet 8: College Planning Worksheet

Use this worksheet to start preparing for your child's higher education. It will help you organize goals, savings, and action steps.

Section	Details/Notes
Student's Name	
High School Graduation Year	
Target Colleges / Universities	
Estimated Annual Tuition & Fees	
Estimated Room & Board	
Other Expenses (books, travel, etc)	
Scholarship Opportunities	
Savings to Date	
Expected Family Contribution (per year)	
Other Funding Sources (529, grants, etc)	
Action Steps (deadlines, applications, etc)	

WORKBOOKS

Retirement Catch-Up Calculator Guide

Many people in the Sandwich Generation feel behind on retirement savings — but it's not too late to get back on track. Use this guide as a step-by-step calculator to see where you stand and how to close the gap.

Step 1: Estimate Your Retirement Goal

- Decide at what age you want to retire.
- Estimate your annual expenses in retirement (housing, healthcare, food, leisure).
  - A simple rule: plan for **70–80% of your current annual income.**
- Multiply that by the number of years you expect to live in retirement (average is 20–30 years).

Example:

- Current income: $80,000
- Target retirement income = 70% = $56,000 per year
- Retirement length = 25 years
- Retirement goal = $56,000 × 25 = **$1.4 million**

Step 2: Calculate Your Current Savings

Add up:
- 401(k), TSP, or 403(b) balances
- IRAs
- Investments (brokerage accounts, CDs)
- Other retirement funds

Step 3: Find Your Gap

Retirement Goal – Current Savings = **Retirement Gap**

Example:

- Goal = $1.4 million
- Current savings = $350,000
- Gap = $1,050,000

Step 4: Maximize Contributions

If you're age **50 or older**, the IRS allows **catch-up contributions**:

- 401(k) / TSP: $23,000 annual max + $7,500 catch-up = **$30,500 per year**
- IRA: $6,500 annual max + $1,000 catch-up = **$7,500 per year**

Even small increases matter. For example:

- Investing an extra $500/month at age 50 can grow to **$150,000+ by age 65** (assuming a 6% return).

Step 5: Run the Numbers

Use an online retirement calculator (from Vanguard, Fidelity, TSP.gov, or NerdWallet) and input:

- Current savings
- Monthly contribution
- Expected retirement age
- Expected investment return (use 5–7% as a conservative estimate)

The calculator will show how close you are and how much more you need to save monthly to meet your goal.

Step 6: Consider Additional Catch-Up Strategies

- Delay retirement by 2–3 years (each extra year reduces the gap significantly).
- Downsize your home and invest the difference.
- Work part-time in retirement to reduce withdrawals.

Review your Social Security benefits and maximize by delaying until age 67–70 if possible.

WORKBOOKS

Item	Amount ($)
Target Annual Retirement Income	
Years in Retirement	
Total Retirement Goal	
Current Retirement Savings	
Retirement Gap	
Annual Savings Needed	
Totals	

Take these figures and plug them into a retirement calculator. The Vanguard calculator is a great simple and free calculator available online. Copy the link below.

https://investor.vanguard.com/tools-calculators/retirement-income-calculator

KEY TAKEAWAY

Catching up on retirement is absolutely possible. The key is to **start now, save consistently, and use every tool available—** including catch-up contributions, smart budgeting, and realistic lifestyle adjustments.

68

CONCLUSION

Looking Back

Throughout this book, we've explored what it means to live in the **Sandwich Generation**:

- The invisible weight of caregiving for children and parents at the same time.
- The cultural expectations and family pressures that shape our decisions.
- The financial juggling act of retirement, budgeting, and estate planning.
- The emotional toll — and the strength — that comes with holding so much together.

We've also discovered practical strategies: setting boundaries, prioritizing retirement, creating family financial playbooks, and designing intentional legacies.

Looking Forward

Being part of the Sandwich Generation is not a sentence to burnout — it's an **invitation to leadership**. You have the chance to:

- Break harmful cycles of financial struggle.
- Teach your children independence and resilience.
- Honor your parents with dignity while still protecting your own well-being.
- Build a legacy that lasts, not just in wealth, but in values and traditions.

This is not just survival. This is the work of **thriving in the middle**.

Your Next Steps

1. **Take one small action this week**. Whether it's starting a family budget, scheduling a retirement contribution, or having a hard but honest conversation, begin now.
2. **Use the worksheets and tools**. They are here to make this journey practical and doable, not overwhelming.
3. **Share what you've learned**. Talk to your children, siblings, and friends. Breaking cycles starts with open conversations.

Final Word

You may sometimes feel pulled in every direction, but remember: you are not alone. Millions share this path — and with planning, boundaries, and courage, you can move from surviving to thriving.

Your legacy is not only what you leave behind. It's how you live today, in the middle of it all, with grace, wisdom, and strength.

The journey of the Sandwich Generation is heavy, but it is also sacred. You are carrying forward **love, duty, and legacy**. This book is not just about survival — it's about thriving, finding strength, and creating a better future.

> "Caring for two generations doesn't mean losing yourself. It means finding the balance between love, responsibility, and your own future."

Thriving in The Middle

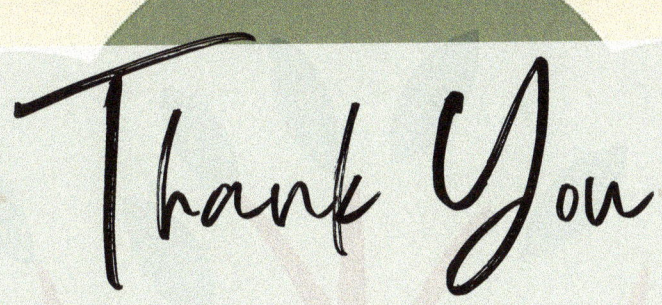

Thank You

A Letter to You, the Reader

Dear Friend,

If you've made it this far, I want to pause and say: **thank you**. Not just for reading these words, but for showing up for yourself, your family, and your future.

I know the weight you carry. I know the quiet sacrifices you make every day that few people see or understand. I know the exhaustion of being "in the middle" — holding up children on one side, parents on the other, while trying not to lose yourself in the process.

But here's what I want you to remember: **you are not invisible, and you are not alone.**

Every page of this book has been written with you in mind — to remind you that your life matters, your dreams matter, and your legacy matters. You are allowed to set boundaries. You are allowed to protect your future. You are allowed to thrive.

The truth is, you are doing sacred work. You are a bridge between generations, carrying forward love, resilience, and possibility. And while that role can feel heavy, it is also powerful.

So take this with you:

- You are enough.
- You are stronger than you know.
- And the steps you take today — no matter how small — are building a future of stability, dignity, and hope for those who come after you.

This is your story, your season, your legacy. Walk forward with courage. You've got this.

With respect and solidarity,
Emily Hutchinson

70

Useful
RESORCES

1

Books & Guides

These books can help deepen your knowledge about family finances, caregiving, and legacy building:

- **"The Other Talk" by Shapiro & Shapiro** – A guide for families about having honest financial conversations.
- **"The Color of Money: Black Banks and the Racial Wealth Gap" by Mehrsa Baradaran** – Understanding systemic barriers to wealth.
- **"Your Money or Your Life" by Vicki Robin** – A timeless guide on reshaping your relationship with money.
- **"The 21-Day Financial Fast" by Michelle Singletary** – A practical reset for financial discipline.
- **"How to Retire Happy, Wild, and Free" by Ernie J. Zelinski** – Retirement planning beyond just the numbers.
- **"In Our Prime" by Susan J. Douglas** – Insightful look at aging, caregiving, and women's roles in midlife.

2

Caregiving & Family Support Organizations

- **AARP Family Caregiving** (aarp.org/caregiving)
  Resources, legal guides, and support for those caring for aging parents.
- **Family Caregiver Alliance** (caregiver.org)
  Advocacy and tools for caregivers, including culturally tailored resources.
- **Eldercare Locator** (eldercare.acl.gov)
  A free government service that connects you with local eldercare resources.
- **National Alliance for Caregiving** (caregiving.org)
  Research and programs focused on family caregiving across the U.S.
- **The Sandwich Generation Network**
  Online support groups and communities for adults balancing kids and parents.

Useful RESOURCES

3 **Financial Planning & Wealth-Building for Communities of Color**
- **National Urban League** (nul.org) – Offers programs in financial empowerment and career development.
- **Prosperity Now** (prosperitynow.org) – Focused on closing the racial wealth gap.
- **Operation HOPE** (operationhope.org) – Free financial coaching, credit building, and small business support.
- **NAACP Financial Freedom Center** – Initiatives around financial literacy and generational wealth.

4 **Mental Health & Caregiver Wellness**
- **Therapy for Black Girls** (therapyforblackgirls.com) – Therapist directory and mental health resources for Black women.
- **Latinx Therapy** (latinxtherapy.com) – Bilingual mental health directory for Latinx communities.
- **National Alliance on Mental Illness** (NAMI) (nami.org) – Support groups and education for caregivers managing stress.

5 **Scholarships & Education Resources**
- **United Negro College Fund** (UNCF) – Scholarships and resources for African American students.
- **Hispanic Scholarship Fund** (HSF) – College funding and resources for Latino families.
- **Jack Kent Cooke Foundation** – Scholarships for high-achieving students with financial need.
- **College Board BigFuture** (bigfuture.collegeboard.org) – Tools to plan, find scholarships, and calculate college costs.

Notes

Notes

Notes